MW01130645

WHEN DEATH

WAS *Calling,*

I DIDN'T

Answer

By

Rhonda Adams

Printed in the United States of America

First Edition, 2022
PAPERBACK ISBN 978-1-0880-7001-7
EBOOK ISBN 978-1-0880-7007-9

Red Pen Edits and Consulting
www.redpeneditsllc.com

DEDICATION

This book is dedicated to three people.

To My Mother, Ms. Idell Flemming. She's my "Shero".

Mom, I dedicate this book to you and say thank you. Thank you for being the example of strength and resilience and for always being my support system. I know life hasn't always been peachy, but you maintained with grace and humility. Through our years, you have displayed the strength of an ox and the importance of not giving up. Mom, you have shared so many examples of creativity and hard work. I can't thank you enough for the endless times you showed up for me and defended me. I apologize for all of the pain I caused by being a disobedient and disrespectful young teen. I didn't want to cause you anymore pain. So, I hid my feelings. I didn't want you to worry about me. So, I tried to figure things out on my own. I made several bad decisions along the way, but your love never changed. Momma, with all the bumps in the road, I'm so grateful to God that he blessed me to have you as my beautiful mother. Thank you for being the one person who always encouraged me to pray. I love you.

To Onik and Kyran

I dedicate this book to the both of you. You are the blessings in the midst of mess that made me choose life. As your mother, I want the absolute best for both of you. I tried hard to be the best example of "no matter the cards dealt, play them and never fold". I apologize for allowing negativity to take residence in my life making me feel like I was better off dead. I pray that this book makes you proud and gives you the strength to fight through your adversities. Throughout life, you will be tested. My prayers are for the both of you to be shielded from all harm. I love you both and want you to know you are not my burdens. You both are my blessings and I thank God for allowing me to be your mother. Onik, you are a handsome king. You will be a good husband and a great father. You are a leader, businessman, homeowner, and a child of God. Remember to pray about everything. Kyran, you are a beautiful queen. Your determining spirit and your future will be big and bright. Follow your heart. Go to college. Make the right decisions concerning your body because you will be a good wife and a great mother. I pray God will shield you from everything that's meant to cause you pain.

I'm so proud of the both of you. Thank you for being the best children. I love you!

TABLE OF CONTENTS

INTRODUCTION

"And ye shall know the truth, and the truth shall set you free." **John 8:32 KJV**

You have just opened a door of truth. In these pages, I will tell you story that is filled with my personal truths. Some of it may seem hard to read. For me, it's even harder to write. The scripture above serves as my premise for writing this book, my truth. I have read many books and memoirs wherein individuals share part, but not the complete truths regarding their past. In order for me to assume this position of a victorious overcomer, I deem it necessary to share from my life experiences for multiple reasons. #1 – You don't have to travel down the same roads and paths that I have traveled. #2 – You can learn from my challenges and live a life of fulfilment that will be more rewarding for you and everyone that you are connected to.

My life is a transparent example of my courageous journey and my pursuit of happiness. I was maneuvering through a dark place called life. Literally, I was lost. I felt alone, embarrassed and hurt. While others actually used illegal drugs, I resorted to sex as my source to get high. Anger could be named of me more than happiness. Depression has a way of creeping into your life and assuming residence without knowing better. I didn't realize how depressed I was until death called my name, "RHONDA!" I'm not talking about a phone call, but I am talking about a distinct voice and life awakening moment that shook me to my core.

Journey with me down memory lane as I share from my childhood and ultimately reveal the powerful, determined, and confident woman that I am today. We all have a story. The purpose of this book is to inspire and help others that are experiencing depression. Depression is real, but God is greater! The United Negro College Fund coined a phrase that said, *"the mind is a terrible thing to waste"*. I would like to elaborate on that concept. If you don't use your mind the correct way, you will leave room for negativity to sow seeds of mediocrity and failure. The mind is a very powerful tool. It is imperative that you use your mind to make better choices. Life happens in many forms. We can't allow our problems to consume us and control our mentality. You have the power to make better life choices and decisions. I have not always made the best decisions, but now, I understand the purpose and truth in every experience of my life. My truths will help you. My truths will set you free. My truths will cause you to realize that through it all, God will always be there. When death called, I didn't answer, and you shouldn't either.

Chapter One

DISRUPTION OF MY CHILDHOOD

Alone. Abandoned. Cold. Empty.

These words can best summate a place of death and dying. In this case, this was a clear depiction of my childhood. I felt as if no one cared for me or even understood me because they were preoccupied with their own lives. I was a lost child in a cold world full of strangers attempting to keep my skeletons hidden. I didn't understand what was happening to me. I was in a continual fight against demons that were suffocating my mind. To me, the actions and appearances of people were different. I was only fourteen, but I faced a lot of opposition. I thought my life was swirling out of control. I didn't like my new address and I HATED my new school!

To add insult to injury, I didn't like what I saw in the mirror. I kept my feelings hidden deep inside. I would pretend to smile. I didn't know how to communicate my feelings, so I was just angry ALL THE TIME! I acquired recognition as the mean, pretty girl. Do you know how they say that your reputation proceeds you? Well, my family hated when I would enter the room because of my attitude. I felt incomplete! I was unhappy most of the time. I was rebellious among so many emotions. Once again, no one cared and that was my cry for help. I was raised to stay in a child's place. It was like one of those "seen and not heard" situations. Communication was limited, especially about our feelings. We just went with the flow of things or so I thought. I didn't understand I was damaged goods. I didn't realize that my mind was unstable because I was numb most of the time. I didn't want the responsibility of being the oldest daughter nor a good student. Because of my attitude and mindset, my grades dropped. I didn't enjoy my high school years as I should have. I didn't experience walking across the stage for my high school graduation. I had to graduate during the summer because I failed English.

(Embarrassment #1)

It started in the summer of 1992. My parents divorced. My two sisters and I eventually spent the summer with my aunt and uncle. My mother never abandoned us. After being a wife for fifteen years, she had to adjust to being a single mother of three young daughters. As the oldest of the three, I had to be a pillar of strength and protection for my two younger sisters. I cried a lot because of the lack of understanding. I didn't know what caused the divorce. I often wondered if I was the reason. I thought my family was good. Even though there were times when things were not so good, I thought that was normal. I remember thinking I'm lucky because my parents were still together when my friends' families were being separated due to divorce.

Then, it happened. I remember coming home from school and being told to have a seat along with my sisters. Our parents said they no longer loved each other and that they filed for a divorce. I remember feeling SHOCKED and CONFUSED! Could I have been a more obedient child? Did I not keep my room clean enough? I had questions. I didn't understand the reasoning for the divorce. I knew change was coming, but not the severity of it. I suggested to my sisters that if we cleaned up and behaved well, that our parents would possibly change their minds and stay together. When my friends' parents divorced, they would come to school crying and acting out. The word "DIVORCE" scared me. My parents said that they loved us and that we weren't the cause of their decision. I still didn't fully understand. I was also frightened as to what was going to happen next.

As time went on, I saw an evil side of my dad. He was very hateful and nasty towards my mom. There was this one time when unplugged a cable from her car to keep her from leaving the house. The person my dad turned into was dark, scary, mean, and hateful. I remember hearing my parents argue and fuss about everything. We just stayed out of their way. One day, when I came home from school, my mother's neck was scratched and bruised. I asked her what happened. She said nothing in a scary, embarrassing tone of voice. My mother has always been the glue to our family. She has the strength of an ox and a love that's unconditional. My dad depended on her a lot when it came to taking care of us and keeping up the house. I'm not saying my dad was all bad, but he could use some improvements with his attitude, pride, and ego.

My parents were strict on being respectful towards others, but during this time, I was seeing the total opposite. I saw a lot of demonic spirits. Many nights, I cried myself to sleep because I was afraid of what was happening. As a child, I didn't want to say or do the wrong thing. Our home lost that warm and fuzzy feeling. It no longer felt inviting. In a quick change of pace, it was turning very cold. As I said before, I didn't understand everything that was going on. My sisters were too young so there is no way that they could fully understand. My mom would often threaten us that we would wake up one day and that she would be gone. That threat scared me to death. I hated hearing her saying that, but in reality, she was very tired. She was tired of being a wife and a mother. I didn't understand the stress level my mom was under. I just wanted things to go back to normal. I wasn't comfortable with the change that had occurred.

Normal for us was an enjoyable experience. When we came home from school, there would be a full meal prepared for us. The house was always clean. Mom was the dominant disciplinarian. My dad worked swing shifts, so my mom spent most of her free time with us. She helped us with our homework, took us to church and spent time with us on the weekends. My mom was also very involved in our school activities where she volunteered a lot. During the holidays, my parents made sure that we had major celebrations. Birthdays were the best. We would gather at the home of a family member for Thanksgiving with the traditional meal, games created memories. We grew closer to our mom's side of the family. My mom had 7 sisters and 8 brothers with 2 sets of twins. We weren't the type of family that showed affections through hugs and kisses, but we knew that we were loved.

I noticed the difference in my parents because I am the oldest. Arguments between my parents became a regular activity. Instead of it happening in private, it happened right in front of us. I felt like my mother didn't feel appreciated or valued. My dad wasn't home as much as we would have liked.

My mom's family was pretty judgmental. Because of that, she had no one to confide in. They thought that she should stay in her marriage for the sake of us. That never works. My mom felt that would be damaging. For so long, the marriage was already over, and the love was not there. That wouldn't improve the situation. I see where I got my stubbornness from - LOL. My parents took on a strong sense of responsibility. Based on this responsibility, they felt compelled to end the marriage and move on. Looking back that was the best decision. Much like most divorces, the transition wasn't an easy one. My dad had pride issues. He felt like he could do whatever he wanted without any repercussions. On the other hand, my mom was afraid. She had to fight to stay alive because of my dad's vindictive, evil ways.

My dad taught us how a man was supposed to treat a woman, but he wasn't demonstrating any of it towards my mom. My dad was sneaky and manipulative; he played the victim in most situations. I didn't like seeing the two of them angry. I was in the latter part of my eighth-grade year and looking forward to the ninth grade. To my surprise, things were not going according to my plan. I didn't realize their decision was going to drastically affect my high school years, but, OH BOY, it did. By this time, we were out of school for the summer and my mother was awarded custody of us. My mom left us with my aunt and uncle until we started school the following school year. I was grateful but still wanted to go back to what I considered my norm. The pain of not being with our mom was unbearable and sad. I remember hearing my grandmother talking with some of my aunts discussing my mother's business. They didn't understand that my mom's actions and decisions were not to be heartless. It's what my mom felt was the right thing to do. My mother wasn't the type to complain or give up; she's a true hustler. My mother always remained positive and hopeful. That summer seemed to be the longest summer ever because we barely spoke to our mom. I would daydream about the day my mom would return to get us from Eastover.

> **Communication is key in family. Instead of gossiping about each other, pray for each other more.**

(Embarrassment #2)

Chapter Two

THE MOVE TO WEST HELL

I can remember when my mom finally came to get us. Her white Toyota was loaded with a lot of our stuff. We pulled into the yard of a little green two-bedroom house that my mom converted into a three bedroom. We walked inside and my mom had the house decorated beautifully. That's one of her many talents. The house was very comfortable and warm. It didn't matter much to me as long as we were all together with our mother. Our mom sat us down and talked to us about the new transition. She also informed us about what she had been doing over the summer in preparation for our return. My mom was very upfront about everything. She had a clever way of protecting us and exposing bits of her life at the same time. My sisters and I never questioned much. We just went with the flow. Our happiness was found in the fact that we were all together again with our mother. My mom never skipped a beat., We always had food, new clothes, and shoes. She kept her bills paid and always had a vehicle to drive. I don't know how she did it, but I'm very thankful for it all. She would work two jobs and didn't complain at all. We were expected to do chores around the house, and she didn't play about that. My mom was a firm disciplinarian, but fair. Oftentimes, she showed her strengths. Rarely would you see her in state of weakness unless she was sick or seriously fatigued. One of those times was when she had to have a hysterectomy. I was helpless during that time and didn't know how to assist her. She endured so much physical pain. I was scared because I didn't want anything to happen to my mother. She was our glue. During my mom's recovery, my sisters and I along with my aunts would take turns helping. I remember some aunts would come and visit to help out as well. My other healed quickly and was back on her grind in record time.

While living in West Columbia, we were forced to grow up quickly. We were sheltered while living in the country. Our neighbors seemed to be nice but going to school was a nightmare. I was judged, bullied and I became depressed. I couldn't understand why the people in West Columbia treated my sisters and I like aliens. I created a hatred for my parents because they got divorced. Because of the divorce, we had to move to West Columbia. High school was supposed to be great. I should have creating lifelong bonds with friends. I was supposed to be going to sporting events. This should be the time where I was making memories. My memories consisted of being hated on, fighting, and cutting school. I met girls who I thought were my friends. They would end up flipping on me because guys would like me more than them. When I came home from school, I would barely express myself to my mom, but she knew I wasn't happy. She encouraged me to keep trying to make friends. I didn't understand what was happening to me. I just know I didn't like it. I took the advice of my mother. I made the JV girls basketball team. I was a part of the chorus, and I participated in the school pageants. I made some new friends, and I had a boyfriend. I used the good advice of my mom, but I was starting to make some bad decisions on my own. The guy that I was dating was older than me and had me sneaking out of the house to see him. Slowly, but surely, I was becoming more and more rebellious. I lost my virginity at age 15 and I had an abortion.

(Embarrassment #3)

This was a great embarrassment for me because I was raised to respect myself and my body. I attended church and Bible study regularly. Some say, "when you know better, you do better." I knew better but was rebellious and disrespectful. I felt like I didn't belong to this new school, and everyone hated me. Instead of talking with my mom and asking for her advice, I felt as if I could handle the pressures. I thought I was protecting my mom by not expressing my pain, concerns, and levels of unhappiness. I was doing more hurt than help. I was actually digging a deeper hole for myself. My mom knew I was pregnant. I lost her trust, but not her love. Even in this, she wanted to teach me that I was too young to be doing adult things. As expected, I was on punishment for a long time. Her advice was for me to love myself and to consider myself to be a prize. She instilled values in me and confirmed my self-worth. She made me understand that most of these guys didn't want to settle down with just me, so I needed to make better decisions. She was right. I learned that the hard way.

I was heading to the 11th grade but making adult decisions with my body. I know I was hurting my mom because I wasn't raised that way. What makes matters worse is that my boyfriend was also sleeping with one of my friends and that had a son together. As a girl, you imagine your first sexual experience to be memorable. For me, it was the complete opposite. Hindsight is 20/20. I should have waited. My mind and body were damaged from that point. For a long period of time, I carried the weight of my high school years. O wish I had communicated with my mother more. By sharing my feelings, she possibly could have directed my life with sound advice.

Communicate to your parents
about everything.

Chapter Three

WHEN I THOUGHT I WAS GROWN

I received my high school diploma during summer school. In high school, I met a good friend that I still know to this day, Miranda. We became more like family. We lived together. We went to family functions together. We worked, fought, traveled, partied together. Two peas in a pod! We were always together. She was even my hairstylist. Boy the memories! She and I were like Thelma and Louise.

We clubbed a lot. One night, while we were out, I saw this guy at the Waffle House who I had met previously. He was so handsome and charming. He came to our table and paid for our food. I remember meeting this guy during our first conversation. I knew he was out of my league. He was wearing an ankle monitor when we met. Even in that, he was persistent and began to pursue me. He found out where I worked and would come to my job. Before I knew it, I found myself doing things that I wasn't taught. I got my first tattoo with him. He was giving me a lot of attention. I didn't realize how much I was changing and none of it was for the good. He introduced me to his world. I was already going to the clubs, but I started going more and more. He had dreams of changing his life and becoming a better man, but his choices didn't line up with those aspirations. Therefore, he was arrested multiple times for making bad decisions. I had never dated someone like him before. He was a sweetheart with a street mentality. He wasn't the ideal boyfriend for me according to my family, but he made me happy. Maybe, I was blind, but this is what I considered to be happiness. I was seeking attention but receiving the wrong attention. Over time, he introduced me to a life of drugs. He taught me how to cook, cut and sell crack cocaine. His advice was to me was that I couldn't be beautiful and not know how to hustle.

(Embarrassment #4)

Throughout this entire time, and not to my knowledge, I was being watched by the police because of my connections with my boyfriend. This same boyfriend is the father to my firstborn.

Chapter Four
WHAT I DIDN'T SEE COMING

Let's recap. By now, I am 20 years old, pregnant, and living with my mom and two younger sisters that were in high school. I was scared, nervous, and mostly embarrassed because I was raised to be married before getting pregnant.
(Embarrassment #5)

Those were the standards that were set from an early age. My son's father was very helpful. Unlike most statistics, he was with me during the entire pregnancy. He was involved in all of my doctor's appointments. On those days when I didn't feel my best, he was right there. However, I noticed some changes in him. I ignored it because I was scared of being alone. I always knew that I wasn't his only woman. Strangely enough, I knew he loved me. Well, at least I hoped he did. He was very protective of me and made me laugh. He was much older. That made me grow up faster. I knew that pregnancy changed women, but I wasn't prepared for the changes in my body. One day, as I looked at the pregnant version of myself, I got really scared. I wasn't prepared to me a mother. I wasn't ready to assume complete responsibility of a child. Would I be a great mom? Time waits for no one. I remember hearing PUSH! I gave birth to a healthy baby boy. That was one of the most emotional days of my life as a young woman. We were blessed. My child was born with all ten fingers and ten toes. His dad was able to cut the umbilical cord. I was so relieved and a little tired. His dad and my mom shared in the celebratory moment and commended me for doing a great job. We were all smiles and talking. All of a sudden, there was silence. I said, "Ya'll! Why my baby not crying? I don't hear anything!" I looked over to my left and there were so many people in the room. I was trying to lift myself out of the bed to find out what was going on. The nurse told me to remain calm. For what? My mom had tears in her eyes. But why? My attitude shifted quickly, and it wasn't in a positive manner. What's going on with my baby? Why isn't anyone saying anything? His dad was crying and hugging my mom. I knew something was going on, but no one was trying to help me understand. During the birthing of a child, there are many expected emotions. Happiness. Jubilance. Cheer. Tears, but of joy. The doctor started explaining to me that the umbilical cord was around my son's neck and restricting his airways. Then, I heard a scream! Ironically, that was the most acceptable scream that I have ever heard. The scream or cry of a newborn baby signified the successful passage of air in and out of lungs. This boy had some strong lungs. His cry meant that he was alive. His cry meant that he was well. His cry was a signal to everyone in the room that he was present and accounted for. One of the nurses laid our son on my chest so he could feel my skin and heartbeat. I was at peace at that moment. The entire mood of the room changed instantly. From fear to freedom. From sadness to happiness. My mom has such a glow on her face because this was the first boy in our immediate family.

Over time, I began to see changes in my son's father. He was less attentive to me, but a good dad to our son. Remember, he was in the drug game. With that, came a lot of other things, such as other women, lies, mixed with mind games and drama.

(Embarrassment #6)

We started fussing and fighting more. I knew I wanted better for myself, so I decided to leave him. He would always make time for Onik, our son. Financially, we were well taken care of. Emotionally and mentally, we were deprived.

(Embarrassment #7)

I didn't realize I was really in a bad place mentally. I was angry a lot because I was allowing money, sex, and the thrill of that lifestyle to corrupt my behavior and my emotions. I didn't see the caliber of hurt and pain in my life until I was out. It's a completely different view from the outside looking in. it was like looking at my life through different lenses. Most times, if you take a few steps back and look again, your perspective will change. Instead of focusing on my personal issues, I consumed myself with work. That took my mind away from what was really important. I didn't realize how empty I was becoming. My mom warned me about losing myself in an effort to make someone else happy. Most people say, "help me, help you." In this case, helping others was hurting me and I didn't understand that concept.

Chapter Five
THE NIGHTMARE CONTINUED

This next phase my life started on a high note. I began my journey of being a single mother to my son. I was concentrating on loving myself again. I finished cosmetology school and received my license. I began working for a hair salon in our local mall. My clientele quickly grew, and the money was coming in like crazy. I enjoyed being a hairstylist because it allowed me to be creative. I loved the expressions on the faces of my clients when the task was completed. The more I worked, the more I learned the business and techniques from the other stylists in the shop. I was trying to date, but my heart wouldn't allow anyone to get close to me because a part of me wanted to believe that my ex and I would figure it out and become a family.

(Embarrassment #8)

Talk about wishful thinking? I had to wake up from the daydream and deal with my reality. This was my reality. Some people enter your life for a reason and others for a season. My ex and I had our season, and we were over. In the process, we created a beautiful baby boy, but together, we were toxic. It was time to face the music. We couldn't be together as a couple. We simply had to co-parent.

My friends and I went to the club a lot. On Wednesdays, we would go to the NCO Club. One Sunday, we were talking about going. I can remember being home on a Monday night and my phone rang. It was my son's dad. He started the conversation with small talk. Then, he went on to say that he needed to talk to me about something. We talked about how we first met and different events that occurred during our relationship. We laughed a lot and then we also cried because he shared some intimate feelings that he was keeping bottled up on the inside. He apologized to me for the hurt he caused. He shared some of his deepest hurt and pain when he had to go back to jail. I vividly remember him saying, "before I go back to jail, I will swallow it first." I felt like he was just talking. It was like he was just caught up in the flow of the conversation. I didn't give it much thought. We were on the phone for hours and honestly, it felt great. It felt great to have a real adult conversation with the man I loved and in actuality, was infatuated with. Tuesday came and we had the same type of conversation. For two nights straight, I had some of the best conversations with my son's father. I felt a beautiful connection between us that I will forever cherish. **(#HappyMemory)**

My homegirl called me early on a Wednesday asking if we were going to the club later that night. My initial response was YES! I got my outfit together and laid it out on the end of my bed. I said I was going to take a little nap to rest before going out, but, for the life of me, I couldn't find rest. My mind was reflecting on the past two lovely conversations that I had with my son's father. I remember calling Miranda and telling her, "No, I'm not going out because I didn't want to see Kino, my son's father." She was trying to convince me to go anyway. I laid back down and something pulled me up out of my bed. To this day, I can't explain what that was, but I felt the pull. It was as if an invisible person was in my bedroom standing over me and pulling me up out of my bed by my arms. I won't lie. I was scared because the pull felt so real. That is something I will never forget. I looked around my room expecting to find someone, but only to realize, I was in there by myself. I got up and called Miranda. I said, "I'm getting dressed." When we arrived at the club, we did our normal - socialized with people we knew and danced. Shortly afterward getting there, I instantly saw Kino. My heart started racing because he wasn't my boyfriend, but there were still feelings there that we both shared. I was standing in line to get a drink. He walked up behind me and grabbed me around the waist whispering in my ear. I pulled away from him. I told him, "I'm not yours anymore. So, stop touching me." Then, I offered to buy him a drink.

He said, "You are not buying me a drink with

another man's money."

I laughed and said, "boy you're crazy."

Then he replied, "we are going home together."

I said, "yea whatever". I felt he was playing games again and he was still caught up in the conversation we had just the night before. So, I paid him no mind. I got my drink and headed to the dance floor to enjoy my night. Every time I would start dancing with someone, he would come to tell the guy that he could not dance with me. I proceeded anyway and I was having a great time. The club was getting ready to close. Kino came up to me and repeated, "I'm going home with you." I laughed, but on the inside, I really wanted him to go home with me. I looked all over for him and asked different people if they had seen him. Everyone said, "no." I ended up going home without him which wasn't a surprise. **(Embarrassment #9)**

I got up the next morning as normal and went to work. I had a full day of appointments. Kino was on my mind all that day. There were multiple times where I dialed his number and hung up before anyone could answer and tell me that he wasn't there. He was known for being with other women. I couldn't understand why he was so heavy on my mind. I brushed it off and went on with my clients. I can remember working on my last client for the day. I rolled her hair and put her under the dryer. I started cleaning my area and finishing up while waiting for my client's hair to dry. The phone rang in the shop. My co-worker answered the phone as I was sweeping the floor. I wasn't paying her any attention until her tone changed and her head dropped. Then, she said, "oh she's right here." She handed the phone to me.

"Hello," I said.

"Girl! Why aren't you answering your phone?"

"I wasn't paying my phone any attention. I'm just trying to get out of here."

She said, "well, I'm coming to get you." I didn't think anything about it. Miranda came flying into the shop with red eyes, crying, and saying, "we have an emergency.

I was asking all kinds of questions because I had never seen her in such an emotional state. "What's going on? Is it my momma? My son? Your momma?" I was so confused.

She said, "No! Just come on, let's go!"

I was beginning to get nervous and scared all at the same time because she wasn't saying much. She asked me to get my things and my coworker said, "Go ahead and go. I will finish cleaning and comb down your client." I thanked her and we left in such a rush. We were running out of the building.

Miranda asked for my keys, and I gave them to her, but not without her telling me what was going before we left the parking lot. I asked her to let me drive because she was shaking like crazy. She looked over to me with tears rolling down her cheeks, shook her head and said, "Kino is dead."
(Embarrassment #10 and hurt)

I immediately got emotional and said, "what?"

She went on to say that someone called her and said that there was a drug bust. Immediately, that didn't line up because Kino wasn't selling drugs. He had a legitimate job. He was working. She went to say that Kino stopped by his momma's house after work and was in the back playing cards. She said someone came by there and within minutes the police pulled up and threw the drugs in Kino's lap. It was too late for Kino to get rid of it. He swallowed the drugs and because of the quality, it burst his heart. The EMS was called because he was getting sick. He was rushed to the hospital. We went to the house first. No one was there. We rushed to the hospital. The first hospital said that no one by the name of Kino was there. We jumped back into my truck and rushed to another hospital. We turned on the road towards the emergency room and there were cars all over the place. Miranda pulled up to the emergency room door. I jumped out and my cousin was there. She opened my truck door and I fell into her arms. By then, I knew that the news I just received was true. I knew my child's father was dead! I remember walking through the halls to get to the room where his family was located. There were people everywhere. I heard a lot of whispers. I saw so many faces. Some familiar. Some unfamiliar. People were crying and inquiring as to what happened. I was a ball of emotions - walking, crying, shocked and full of disbelief. I arrived too late, so I was unable to view his body. While in the room with the family, we cried, and I was trying to get myself together. I got so sick. I began sweating. My stomach was in knots and then I began to vomit. There were so many thoughts that ran through my head. I was beating myself up because I wish I had allowed the phone to ring until someone answered when I called him earlier. Maybe he would've come to my job and not his parents' house. There were so many questions.

Kino's dad pulled me to the side and said, "Rhonda, my son was asking for you the whole time while were in the back of the ambulance. He said to tell you that he loved you before he took his last breath." His dad went on to say that he didn't say anything about a message to anyone else - just you. I know his dad was hurt because he was with his child during his last minutes on earth. I can only imagine how hard that could be.

Hours had passed in the hospital. I was staring at the wall while rocking back and forth in the chair. My heart was racing. People were talking to me but, I heard nothing. My cousin, Kia, was with me the entire time. Miranda was there as well. She split her time with me and in the family room. A local pastor came into the room and prayed with us. The tears were flowing like a waterfall from a mountain. In that moment, I knew that my life had changed, but I didn't know to what extent. How was I going to tell my son that his dad was gone and not going to be back? How would he receive that information? The family was in so much pain. I wanted to change the outcome of that day. I completely numb emotionally. As the crowd lessened, I was convinced to leave to go get some rest.

The next morning, I expected to wake up from the nightmare of the previous day. In order to sleep, my mother gave me some medicine that caused me to be in a daze. Now, came the time to break the news to my son. Due to the genuine creativity of my son, the conversation went like this. My son equated his father's death similar to his baby turtle.

"Oh my God! Yes, son! Just like your baby turtle," I explained.

"Do we have to have a funeral for him?" my son inquired.

"Yes, baby." I responded.

Then, came the hard question. "Mommy, how did my daddy die?"

I knew that my son, as smart as he is, would process the information in his own creative way. "Your dad swallowed drugs that were the size of a cookie, and it caused problems for his heart." My son was only four years old, so he thought that all cookies were bad. He went through the kitchen and threw away all of the cookies. Telling my son the truth was necessary but at the same time so hard that it made me sick for days. Kino's mother called everyday requesting for her grandchildren to be with her. This was hard for me because they were so phony to me. I had to force myself to go over there. We went to the club every night leading up to his funeral because that's what he did. Every night, I would get drunk and high to the point that I couldn't feel a thing.

(Embarrassment #11)

There were many different scenarios as to what led up to Kino's death. To this day, I still don't know the whole truth. As of this writing, I have a twenty-three-year-old that I am proud to call son. That death took a major mental toll on my life. I gained weight and alcohol was my coping mechanism. Being a mother wasn't something that I took seriously.

(Embarrassment#12)

I felt like a failure in every area of my life. I didn't like the pain I was feeling. I didn't understand why my sons' father had to die. I was so hurt and just wanted to protect my son. I carried the weight of the hurt and didn't allow anyone to get close to me. One of the worst parts was that I didn't talk about my hurt. Sometimes, it takes a simple conversation to relieve yourself of unnecessary pain and anguish. I felt like I was dying inside. Suicide felt like the easiest way to rid myself of the mental strain. One night, I reserved a hotel room and contemplated ways to end my life. I cried so hard that I was vomiting every hour on the hour. From taking pills to smoking weed to drinking lots of alcohol, I did everything that I could end my life. Maybe, I would just die in my sleep. I felt empty, alone, confused and I didn't see myself as being a good mother to my son. In that moment, I allowed the enemy to control my thoughts and actions. I allowed the spirit of doubt and fear to take control of my life. When I woke up the next day, it was late in the afternoon. I was so sick and barely alive, but alive. I tried my best to end my life and failed. If death did come knocking on my door, I didn't answer. If death had called me, I didn't answer. I was alive! However, my energy was at an all-time low. I had given up on life. I was angry with God for taking Kino. I felt this way because I was raised to have a husband, not a child and no husband. I was so embarrassed.

(Embarrassment #13)

After a few months went by, I used work to keep me busy. That was my way of not focusing on the hurt. My sense and emotions were a wreck, but I could see the true intent of so many people around me. I didn't feel like people were being genuine in asking about me and my son. The "are you ok" messages lacked concern and substance. It was really weird. They weren't truly concerned about our feelings.

Emotions have a way of reflecting in your daily activities and showing up outwardly. I gained a lot of weight during this time. Food was happy and safe place. I can remember shopping for an all-black outfit for an event. It got so bad that I found myself crying in the fitting room of a department store because my clothing size had increased to sizes 22 and up. I was having a mental breakdown. I had never been that size before. I found it ironic that the people that were around me the most never brought it to my attention that I was getting bigger. However, the store clerks and some customers were my saving grace. They came and checked on me. Talk about angels in disguise. They spoke life and encouragement into my life. I had to make a life decision. I got myself together and contacted a trainer to assist in my wellness journey. Over the next five months, I lost the extra weight. This is how I gained the necessary strength and confidence for the next chapter of my life.

Chapter Six

MR. RIGHT WAS ACTUALLY MR. WRONG

As years went by, I kept up with my weight loss journey and started dating again. It was one failed relationship after another. I wouldn't allow a man to get close to me because I was afraid of him dying as well. I carried that fear for a very long time. I began working at this urban clothing store that was known for having customers that were ballers, celebrities, and dope boys. I was hesitant about working there because I never worked in a clothing store. After a few weeks of training, I made a great impression and became a store manager. I was so proud of myself. I started to live again. Working there opened me up to many perks and bonuses like tickets to the comedy shows, concerts and other special event opportunities with VIP treatment. I adopted the name "Red" when I worked there.

One day, this man with a chocolate skin complexion walked in asking for a store manager that was off that day. I spoke with the gentleman and offered to assist him, but he politely declined. I complete understood because there were some customers that chose to deal with specific people in the store. This guy looked like a businessman and had his stuff together. I wanted to know who he was. While out with some friends, this same guy walked in with a mutual friend. We made eye contact in a flirting manner. Our mutual friend took the initiative to say that he was curious about me. Back then, I had a quick and slick tongue. Immediately, I advised my friend to allow this guy to speak for himself. Soon after, he came over with small talk and brought drinks for the table. At the end of the night, he gave me his number. I didn't want to seem desperate, so I didn't call him for a few days. I was kinda dealing with someone off and on, but as I said before, I didn't want to get too close to anyone. I decided to finally use his number. I was nervous at first because I didn't know if he would remember me. From his end, he was wondering if I was ever going to call him.

After talking over the phone for a few weeks, he invited me to ride with him to Charlotte for lunch and a shopping spree. I should have paid more attention. I was caught up in the difference of how he was playing me. He was an older guy and very smooth with his words and actions. On top of that, I was captivated by the attention that he was giving me. There were red flags everywhere and I was oblivious to them all. In a matter of months, I moved into this guy's house. I was so confused. I really thought that I was in love and that he really loved me. Even though I noticed differences in the relationship, I still accepted his proposal of marriage and we moved to Charlotte. While planning our wedding, we found out that we were pregnant. I was full of emotions. I remember being so excited. The house had three levels, seven bedrooms, five and half bathrooms, laundry room, office space, living room, den, a bonus room with a deck and a studio in the basement where the children would play. My son lived there, but his children visited often.

My vision of my life was beginning to turn dark again. Since I was pregnant, my emotions and feelings were all over the place. I blamed it on my hormones. As time went on, our relationship began to feel more like roommates than an engaged couple. I was suffocating my pain to protect his feelings and to keep peace. In order to eliminate the emotions of pain and anguish from my unborn child, I chose to not participate in any arguments. There were many nights when I would get in the jacuzzi tub and cry my eyes out. One of the most hurtful things was when I would tell him about my doctor appointments well in advance only to have him provide another excuse as to why he couldn't make it. **(Embarrassment #14)**

I was still working in Columbia. Through the grapevine, I began hearing about his cheating, but I didn't have any hard evidence. My embedded woman's intuition caused me to feel as if something was wrong. He stopped communicating. He stopped touching me. He stopped complimenting me and making time for me. Things were changing drastically. When I had to work, I would stay at my mom's house. My son would stay with him in Charlotte because he had school. I was between seven and eight months pregnant. I remember laying in the bed and the baby (a girl) was moving so much in my stomach. I was restless. I remember reading the bible and praying over my relationship that night. After tossing and turning, I went downstairs to the second level to the kitchen. I fixed something to drink in hopes that she would calm down so I could get some rest. I sat at the kitchen table and the phone started to ring. I didn't rush to get it in hopes that he would answer it in the studio. The phone continued to ring. I finally got up and answered the phone.

Me: "Hello?"

Caller: "Hey, is such and such there?"

Me: "Yes, he's in the studio. May I have asked who's calling?"

Caller: "Can you tell him this is his girlfriend?"

She left her name. I replied, "Hello girlfriend. I'm Rhonda, the fiance!" As you could imagine I was immediately pissed, hurt, betrayed, and embarrassed! I asked her to please hold on. I'm took the phone to him. I was huge and pregnant, but I shot down the stairs like a bullet. I burst inside the studio snatching the door wide open with a room full of people. He didn't realize I had the phone on speaker call. I said, "Here! Your girlfriend is on the phone."

He laughed and said, "what?"

I repeated, "she said she's your girlfriend named _____. That's funny because we are engaged!" I then heard her voice screaming his name. I threw the phone and stormed out of the studio. I heard people screaming to get Rhonda. She's pregnant. I flew up the stairs. He was right behind me and grabbed me. I was fighting him off of me. I didn't want him to touch me. I cursed him out so bad! I was an emotional wreck. I was already feeling lonely, but to have everything confirmed was a reality a reality that I didn't want to face. For days, I refused talking to him. I kept myself isolated. My blood pressure was sky high. I was eventually put on bed rest because I was a high-risk pregnancy. I couldn't stand the sight of him. I didn't deserve to be lied to the way he did. I felt the whole relationship was based on lies. I was mad at myself for getting pregnant again and allowing someone to get that close to me, just to hurt me. I had a child that was created with a man who really only cared about himself. Here's the most embarrassing thing. I'm a black woman in a relationship with a black man who was cheating with a white woman. My insecurities and my lack of confidence were at an all-time high. My heart would cringe when thinking about all the red flags that I failed to acknowledge.

(Embarrassment #15)

Day in and day out, I cried. I can remember him saying that he was sorry and that he wanted to make it right. Contrary to that attempted apology, he would say, "damn, you're always crying!" No emotion. No remorse. I thought that was so dumb. Here I was, thinking that someone could actually love me and want to marry me, but now I am a single mother again, but with two children. There was no way I was going to marry a man knowing he was being unfaithful. When it got closer to my due date, my mother came to Charlotte to be with me. He traveled a lot, so he was rarely there. My mother and I decorated the baby's room. That's something that he and I should have done. Hindsight is 20/20. Looking back, I realized that he was only old based on age because his actions were very childish. His idea of security, love and affection were in paying the bills and showering me with gifts. None of that could replace happiness and peace of mind. He had me figured out wrong. I wanted the things that money couldn't buy. I wanted to feel the security, love, and respect. I wanted him to desire me and only me. When I gave birth to our daughter, he was there and seemed very excited. I had our daughter in the hospital in Columbia and we stayed at my mom's house for a couple of weeks before returning to Charlotte. I hoped things were going to get better between us for the sake of our daughter, but it wasn't consistent. I felt myself sinking into a deep depression. This led to a second suicide attempt.

There was a very sharp, narrow curve on the road before turning into our neighborhood. We got into a very heated argument. I stormed out the house and jumped into the car while crying and talking to myself. While speeding up the road, I headed towards the curve in hopes of going over the edge. Visions of the relationship started flashing through my mind. I was so mad. My heart was racing. I felt like I was having a heart attack. My head was pounding. I was shaking like a leaf on a tree on a windy day. I was driving so recklessly. I remember approaching that sharp curve doing at least 120 mph. My car stopped suddenly right before tipping over the cliff. I instantly felt like I woke up from a nightmare.

A random lady came over to my car. She said that she saw me for a while and praying for me and my safety. She thought something was wrong with my car. Frantically, I was crying because she had no idea that I was trying to take my life. There she was, praying for me as if she was a guardian angel. After getting myself together, she helped to get my car off the cliff with no damage. I didn't realize I was gone for so long. He said that he was calling my phone. He claimed that he wanted his family. My eyes and heart were privy to any of those efforts. I decided to leave him. Our daughter was about two months old. I came back to Columbia. After a while, I started back doing hair again. Slowly, but surely, I regained my strength.

Chapter Seven
THE TURN OF EVENTS

One of my purposes in life is to make an indelible impression in the lives of my two children. At this point in my life, I wanted a major change for my children. Looking back over my life, I was very displeased with my way of living. Many times, I wanted to give up and stop living. I hated myself for years. When I looked in the mirror, I was disgusted at the image of who I had become. My heart's sentiments cried out for a change from. God. Death tried to call me on so many different occasions. I attempted suicide twice and survived transported drugs. I was in the midst of multiple shoot outs. I was arrested. I almost had a stroke. I used my body for the temporary satisfaction of love. I had many financial issues. BUT GOD!!

God kept me! Even in my foolish decisions, God loved me more than I loved myself and when I didn't love myself. He had his hand on me the entire time. I felt like I had a purpose, but I didn't understand it at that time. I began to attend church more. I sought to understand my journey and the wholeness of my purpose. One day while praying, I asked God to show me what he has in store for my life. I was so tired of crying and not feeling worthy. I didn't want to be known as Rhonda, the mean and nasty person with a cold heart. I've always wanted to help others and make a positive impression in their lives. I just didn't know the level of help that I needed. I was ready to seek direction. I cried out to God to change and help me. I desired more out of my life, and it was revealed to me in a dream. In the dream, I saw the words "Eye Told You". I didn't fully understand what that meant. After seeking God for more and attending church, I gained more of an understanding about "Eye Told You".

I would often talk with my mother about things that bothered me and things I wanted to change in myself. Her answer would always be for me to pray and seek God for all understanding. I did just that! While taking a nap that same afternoon, I had a dream and it seemed so real. It was a beautiful, sunny day. I was on stage speaking to a massive audience of men, women, and children from various ethnicities. I don't recall the overall concept of the event, but I assume it was about me and my purpose. The attendees were wearing t-shirts of different colors that read "Eye Told You". I distinctly saw the words and the logo. Love was being displayed through smiles and tears of joy. The people were fellowshipping with each other, taking pictures, eating, and dancing. It was an enjoyable time. There were familiar faces and some faces that I didn't recognize. I asked God "What does the eye told you mean"?

He spoke to me so clearly. "I need you to share your story and your untold truth to help others. The 'Eye' is what you use to see. It represents your vision. I foresee you being great at helping and encouraging others. The 'Told You' gives you the responsibility of your own destiny. Regardless of the roads traveled and the potential obstacles, you kept the faith and overcame the odds." God said, "don't be afraid! Trust me!"

At that time, I still didn't fully understand, but I started. I wrote words that spoke life to me and even talked to myself in the mirror to start each day. I prayed to God for exactly what I wanted. I was being more patient, open, helpful, and loving towards others. I began to take a more positive outlook on my life instead of gravitating to the negative. I began to walk with my head held high, shoulders back, and posture straight. I started owning the rooms I entered by smiling more and frowning less. To some, these gestures may seem minor, but for me, it was something huge.

I was the person that would cry myself to sleep at night. I felt lonely and alone even when I was in a relationship. I was the mother that felt like a failure. I couldn't always give my children what they wanted, but God always supplied our needs. Smiling more and crying less was a major accomplishment for me and signified moving in the right direction.

I was very selfish in trying to end my life because of the choices I made and the actions that followed. Now my actions and outcomes are much better.

I have events such as fashion shows with a twist (beautiful message). I ask for models that have overcome adversities in their lives and walk boldly in their truths. These events are created for entertainment purposes, but with an understanding that change is needed in their minds and life. Reach One! Teach One! That's the transformative message.

The memories that have been made with my children are heartfelt and priceless. We have to understand that making small positive steps in the right direction speaks volumes. The most important part is not stopping. Keep pushing, keep fighting and understand you are not alone. The battle is not yours. It's the Lord's. Put your trust in him. I'm a product of a praying family. The key is to pray myself through situations that I face. Through life, I lost faith, but I also knew it was important for me to gain it back. This also applies to you. You have to make the decision to not stay stuck in your darkness.

For me, it started by writing my goals and speaking them into existence. I believe I am better than my past. My mindset has changed. Prayer has a way of relieving you of pain, weight, and burden. Things were changing for the better. There's an old adage that says, "the things that I use to do, I don't do anymore. The places that I use to go, I don't go anymore." My tastes and preferences were changing. Cravings that I once had were fading away. I wanted to be in more positive environments. I wanted to be in the light rather than darkness. This process has taken years. It doesn't happen overnight. Trust me! There will be challenges along the way. I made the decision to step out on faith and become a better person. Now, I understand that I was created for a purpose and to rush things to meet my personal deadlines. God has my attention and is still positioning me by sending the right people my way to encourage me. I have been in a lot of toxic relationships where the men have used, abused, and taken advantage of me. I have had friendships that died and family members that treated me like a stranger. I previously thought that I needed to have a man to be complete. That was the work of the enemy. That kept me from my divine purpose and the plan that God had for my life. Daily, I remind myself that I have a bright future. Daily, I motivate myself so I can effectively encourage others. Daily, I consider the scripture as written in Jeremiah 29:11 (KJV) where it says, "For I know the thoughts that I think toward you, saith the Lord, thoughts of peace, and not of evil, to give you an expected end."

I am confident that things are working and turning in my favor according to Psalms 57:2 KJV.

"I will cry unto God most high; unto God that performeth all things for me."

Chapter Eight
MY HEART TALK

Have you ever heard the saying that "hurt people, hurt people"? We have to understand that broken people don't realize the extent to which they are broken. Furthermore, they don't care about the hurt they bestow on others. I believe in reciprocation. That said, I'm constantly praying for others as well as myself. I pray God will bless me with a husband that can handle all of me. I pray for a long healthy marriage and life. I pray that others seek and find the type of peace that money can't buy. I pray for the type of happiness that comes with a peace of mind that God will always provide and will always be there for you, even if you are broke and on your dying bed. I pray that my mother is proud of the woman that I've become. I pray that my children are proud of me as their mother and learn from my lessons without going down the paths that I previously traveled. I pray that my sisters understand that the pain I carried for years wasn't because of anything they did to me, but the repercussions of my choices. I pray that you all understand that you have choices to make in life. It's imperative to make the right decisions. You may not get a second chance to right your wrong. I have done things that are not right, but my heart is big. There are many keys to success written within the lessons of the stories that you are reading. One of those keys is that you can overcome anything you put your mind to. Life is full of roller coasters. Are you going to pray for protection during the ride or not take the ride at all out of fear? My role is to be a positive light in the lives of other people. Each day, I decide to rise above. I was divinely chosen to use my voice and life experiences to motivate and mold the minds of others that have lost their will to fight. My current job has turned into a rewarding ministry tool. I am afforded an opportunity to use my life experiences, struggles, and triumphs to encourage patients. I also get to share with my coworkers. I understand that my message will not be received by everyone. For those that choose to listen, I will make myself available. I choose to tell me testimony. I choose to live. I didn't answer when death was calling because my purpose to live was more important.

Chapter Nine

STOP PLAYING WITH YOUR POTENTIAL

I feel like sharing my journey to take control of my life is an obligation. Someone has been waiting to hear my story and read this book. My desire to see change in my life began with me speaking things into existence. I prayed for a better life. I isolated myself from familiar places and situations because I knew I was weak. I didn't want to tempt myself and be influenced by the very thing that I was praying for deliverance from. Depression rates have recently escalated. One out of four Americans will suffer from some type of depression in their lives. There's no quick fix!

I learned how to manage my depression by doing things that made me happy. I would exercise and share my feelings with my family more. That helped me become more vocal and less moody. Compulsive eating was another challenge for me. When I was depressed, I would eat. The worst part is that I would eat the wrong types of food. Because of this, I was gaining more and more weight. By substituting healthier foods for bad foods, I slowly changed my eating habits. I find myself smiling more because I see a positive reflection of myself in the mirror. It feels good to smile instead of drowning myself in my pillow filled with tears. I decided to live a happier, healthier life. I smile instead of frown. I pray instead of worrying. I appreciate the simple things instead of taking them for granted.

It didn't feel good to lose long time friendships, but if they no longer added value to my life, I had to move on. People and conversations that drained me or left me unmotivated, were a threat to my potential and greatness. You have to prevent connecting yourself with toxic people. If you connect with them, you run the risk of having their negative characteristics and traits to transfer to you. Carrying their negativity and your personal challenges is unnecessary. Toxic energy is contagious. Isolation has been beneficial to me. By protecting my surroundings, I was able to rebuild my self-love and self-esteem. Because of that decision, I was able to take control of myself and my happiness.

I love myself! In times past, I put others before me. It's nice to do for others. It's great to be selfless, but there is a time to be selfish on purpose. Boundaries are important. You have to be intentional about what you will and will not accept. Your mental capacity and state are just as important as your physical. You are not a trash receptacle. Don't allow people to dump their mess on you. Everyone doesn't live based upon the golden rune to "treat others how you want to be treated". Some people are only connected to you because they know that they can get something out of you or solely based on the benefit you are to them. This should raise a red flag to you. Be very aware. Create safe zones and proper distance. It is ok to "love people from afar". I love to listen to people so I can provide the appropriate help without judging. When I began loving myself more, I built my confidence. I started being more vocal about my life and experiences. I have a story to tell. I don't share my story for pity or sympathy. My story is told to encourage others and be an inspiration to many.

About The Author
~ Rhonda Adams ~

Rhonda Adams is the proud mother of two (son and daughter) wonderful and beautiful children. Adams was born in Hopkins, SC, but later moved to West Columbia after the divorce of her parents in 1991. She is an Alumnus of Brookland Cayce High, graduating in 1996. She attended the Kenneth Shuler School of Cosmetology and became licensed as a cosmetologist in 2000. Rhonda currently lives in Columbia, SC and employed by Lexington Medical

Center as a Patient Access Representative and leader over her department.

For several years, pain, darkness, and emptiness existed in her life through bullying from others, depression, and suicidal attempts. Becoming a single parent at an early age was not easy. At the age of four, her son lost his father due to a drug overdose. Not knowing how she was going to raise her son alone, Rhonda became confused and lost. Because of this pain, her life began to spiral out of control. Life was like playing rushing roulette in not knowing or caring about the consequences that she may face. Rhonda eventually moved out of her mother's house, leaving her son behind in hopes of defeating the challenges of life and in an attempt to get her life in order. As time passed, she became involved in toxic relationships, experienced weight increase, and eventually had a mental breakdown. Life was numb. Rhonda began to suffocate her pain with negative feelings and behaviors, not realizing the harm she was inflicting upon herself.

As time passed, Rhonda decided to return to

her mother's house to live and become closer to her son. She later became involved in a promising relationship and moved to North Carolina. The union of this relationship brought forth the blessing of her daughter. The relationship became toxic leading to multiple failed suicidal attempts. The relationship ended and she returned to South Carolina.

After returning to South Carolina, Rhonda continued her career as a hairstylist and a counselor at her local church. As a counselor, she began to share the untold truths about her life by helping others to understand that everyone has a story to tell. By confessing the truth about her life, she has deterred others from committing suicide and encouraged removing themselves from toxic relationships. The ability to share her failures and triumphs with all sexes, races, and nationalities has allowed individuals to gain strength, courage, and realize no one has to face their challenges alone. There are others like them, and we stand together as one. We must seek God, pray harder, believe in ourselves, and surround ourselves with positivity.

Rhonda's sharing of her life obstacles and triumphs has led to the development of the Eye Told You Movement of which she is the founder and CEO. The motto of the Eye Told You Movement is "in spite of the road traveled, see the road ahead." The Eye Told You Movement inspires individuals to change the current vision of themselves and see a positive reflection that lies ahead. The Eye Told You Movement holds speaking seminars for individuals or groups to inspire any population never to give up. Since 2018, we have hosted numerous fashion shows that depict a story about everyday life situations. The fashion show represents how we are models of our life's truths, and that it is okay to feel hurt as long as you do not become complacent with feeling hurt.

Rhonda aspires to be a world-known motivational speaker and the CEO of multiple businesses instilling positive energy, self-love, and the ability for others to become successful at achieving their goals despite the history of their past. Rhonda challenges everyone to set and achieve goals regardless of their past. History should not be a repeat of itself but a way to achieve a positive future for yourself.

For More Information About Rhonda Adams and the Eye Told You Movement:

Follow Rhonda Adams on Facebook

Follow Eyetoldyou_movement_ceo on Instagram

Call: 803-800-0840

Email: eyetoldyou1@gmail.com

Printed in the USA
CPSIA information can be obtained
at www.ICGtesting.com
LVHW060640250124
769631LV00031B/362

9 781088 070017